Marie-Odile and Jean Plassard

VISITING ROUFFIGNAC CAVE

Photographs by Marie-Odile and Jean Plassard

Translated by Angela Moyon

SUD OUEST

This is the largest complete mammoth in the cave and it is doubly interesting. The outline has been drawn with one finger, in a single sweep from trunk to hind leg, a fine demonstration of the "professionalism" shown by prehistoric artists, and it only has one tusk which seems to be hard up against a small piece of flint (Length = 1.35 metres / 4 ft. 4 ins)

When you leave Les Eyzies, the Capital of Prehistory, take the road northwards, following the signposts to Périgueux. Wending its way through forests of oak and chestnut, the road will take you slowly upwards onto the plateaux at Rouffignac. There, three miles to the south of the village, is the Légal Plateau. The steeply sloping sides of this Campanian limestone upland topped by a thick layer of iron-bearing clay stand some 357 ft. above the Binche Valley to the east and the Malestride Valley to the west. It is on the slope above the Binche that, hidden amongst the oaks, yawns the low, dark mouth of the Cro de Granville

The hillside, the valleys to each side of it, the clay that covers it, the limestone that forms its base, and the cave within it are all part of a long succession of geological and prehistoric events. From the beginnings of the cretaceous sea eighty million years ago to the Iron Age burial grounds of one hundred and thirty centuries ago, we are faced with a veritable enigma. In the next few pages, we shall try to describe the main events in this wonderful adventure and help you to pick out the principle pointers to the past.

AN OLD ACQUAINTANCE

Beneath the scorching sun of the early summer months, four men entered the mouth of the Cro de Granville cave that had formed a gash in the hillside since time immemorial. Their shadows lengthened and became distorted as their footsteps became heavier, weighed down by the clay sticking to their shoes.

Five, six hundred yards, and the cave walls became smoother; the cave roof was lower and flatter. The heavy acetylene lamp was lifted higher and the light flickered across the whitish chalk. Engravings appeared. The visitors caught their breaths and, in a silence broken only by the hiss of the lamps, the outlines of two mammoths appeared. It was June 26th 1956 and the Rouffignac Cave had just entered the history books.

From mammoth to rhinoceros, from rhinoceros to horses, ibex and bison, slithering across the bears' dens, craw-ling along a gallery that in some places had a very low roof, Professor L.R. Nougier, R. Robert, and C. and L. Plassard discovered more than one hundred examples of Paleolithic art in the feverish explorations of those first few hours.

Yet those who had discovered the prehistoric art in Rouffignac did not know about the cave itself. For centuries past, countless visitors had passed through this maze. It was François de Belleforest, in his work entitled "Cosmographie universelle" published in 1575, who first described the "Miremont grotto". "Near Miramont too, a small town in Périgord, there is a cavern or grotto known to the local people as a "cluzeau", of which those who have entered it recount great wonders... and it contains a few altars, and paintings in several places, and the trace or mark of footprints of several types of great beasts and small animals..." This text, and many others, form milestones in the cave's history.

Alas! Most of the "tourists" of earlier centuries were not satisfied with merely satisfying their curiosity. Most of them, usually accompanied by a local who served as a guide, marked their visit by writing their name and, in many cases, the date of their visit on the cave wall or roof with the smoke from their candles. Unfortunately, these four centuries of unrestricted visits resulted in some damage to the cave and anybody who comes to see it today suffers the consequences - the visitors of centuries past have covered many of the Paleolithic paintings with graffiti. The rediscovery of the prehistoric art marked the end of this long period of damage and, thanks to swift action on the part of the French Monuments Historiques (the equivalent of the National Trust), access to the cave was restricted and protection was ensured.

Thereafter, speleologists and prehistorians called upon specialists such as geologists or paleontologists for assistance. After long periods spent underground and, in some cases, a number of veritable sporting feats, thirty-five years of observation, inventory, measurements, and analyses have resulted in extensive know-

Bears' dens. These numerous lairs shaped by the bears tend to suggest the existence of a colony but this was not the case. It was merely the repetition of the same behaviour over several tens of thousands of years that led to this large number of hollows. They range in diameter from 1.50 - 2.50 metres / 5 - 8 ft.

ledge of the cave and its contents.

Luckily, today's visitors no longer need to crawl nor climb to see the natural and archaeological features of this prehistoric site. A small electric train makes the art work accessible to as many visitors as possible, while preserving it in the best possible conditions.

THE FORMATION OF THE SUB-TERRANEAN PASSAGES

The Cro de Granville, now known as the Rouffignac Cave, forms a maze with some six miles of galleries in three storeys, one above the other. Only the upper storey, by far the largest of the three, was explored and frequented by the prehistoric artists. Its layout is reminiscent of a tree devoid of all but its main branches. It

is the end of one of these "branches", which forms a wide opening onto the outside world, that forms the only possible entrance to the network of passageways. A geological and topographical survey of the cave has shown that the layout was identical in the Paleolithic Era. In fact, the cave we see today is identical to the cave of prehistoric times. It consists of a series of vast galleries, most of them wider than they are high, set out to each side of the main passageway in a herring-bone pattern. In some places, the ground, which is covered with a thick layer of clay, is strewn with slabs of rock that have fallen from the roof or cave walls.

The walls themselves bristle with numerous flint modules, while huge natural domes break up the monotony of the vaulted roof. Only the very last "twigs" formed by successive subdivi-

sion of the branches remain inaccessible because they are too narrow and the roofs too low. Because the arrangements made for tourists concern only the main galleries, the site has not lost any of its natural appearance and geological observations all remain feasible.

Its high topographical situation, which is rare in this area, means that the cave consists of a chalky limestone rich in clay and flint, i.e. "campanian" limestone. Some eighty million years ago, during the Cretaceous Era, numerous layers of sediment were deposited at the bottom of the sea. The rare feature of this upland is that it remained almost unaffected by the movements of the earth's crust and the settling caused by its own mass. Because of this, the vertical fractures (or diaclases) that are usually found in this type of rock are fairly infrequent

The engraving of the First Mammoth. It owes its name to the fact that it was the first piece of art work discovered by L.R.Nougier, R. Robert and C.L. Plassard on 26th June 1956 (Length = 85 cm / 2 1/2 ft).

here. The hollowing process took place on a horizontal plane, along the stratographical joints. As in all natural networks of underground passages, it was water that hollowed out the galleries. It began its work at the end of the Secondary Era, some seventy million years ago. Initially, it set up a chemical reaction. Water seeped in from the outside through a large vertical crack leading up to the plateau, known as the "aven". Permeating the stratographical joints, it decomposed the chalk, thereby freeing the insoluble clays that slowly piled up along the bottom of the gallery. This means that the network was hollowed out and filled in simultaneously, and the process continued throughout the Tertiary Era (65 million years).

It was not until the start of the Quaternary that the gallery gained its present appearance. The fairly abrupt hollowing out of the valley floors caused much of the filling to be sucked out while the water, which was drawn towards the deeper diaclases, dug out the lower storeys. In fact, these lower passageways still contain a stream to this day. While the lower storeys gradually drained off the water, the upper passageways dried out, and the unused aven was blocked up naturally. Only the present entrance, the point at which the water originally gushed out of the cavern, remained open, like a yawning hole. Animals and man could now take possession of the site.

VISIBLE PROOF OF THE ACTION OF THE WATER

Just a few yards into the cave, strangely-shaped stones draw the visitors' attention - the flint modules. These concentrations of silicon envelopped in a limestone husk have withstood the action of the water. The outer shell was porous and became impregnated with the iron oxydes that were dissolved in the water. This is why they look red on the walls and roof of the cave.

Because of variations in the quality of the chalk, it offered varying degrees of resistance to the water, as is most obvious from the terraces on the cave walls.

The roof is decorated with vast domes. Unequal degrees of resistance in the rock caused rockfalls which resulted in irregularly-shaped cavities which were rounded and polished by the chemical and mechanical action of the water. Often, pot-holers describe these domes as upturned cauldrons or pressurised cauldrons.

DATES B.P.	PERIODES	DECORATED CAVES AND ROCK-SHELTERS IN FRANCE
3000 5000 10 000	Historic Metal age Neolithic Mesolithic	
12 000	Late Magdalenian	Teyjat
13 000		**ROUFFIGNAC** Bernifal Font de Gaume Combarelles Saint-Cirq
15 000	Middle Magdalenian	Bédeilhac Niaux Cap Blanc
17 000	Lower Magdalenian	Lascaux Bara-Bahau Villars Cougnac Pech-Merle
19 000	Solutrean	Pataud Le Poisson
23 000	Gravettian	Pair-Non-Pair Cosquer Gargas
30 000	Aurignacian	

The position of the Rouffignac Cave in the chronologie of decorated caves and rock shelters.

The Great Pit *(part of the frieze). Professor Leroi-Gourhan's observations revealed that certain species, especially horses and bison, were depicted together in several different works. In Rouffignac, there are six combined mammoth/bison pictures. The frieze in the Great Pit is a particulary fine example of this feature (Length = 70 cm/2 ft. 2 m).*

ANIMALS PRECEDED MAN

As the train moves slowly forward, its headlights flicker across the walls of the cave. In many places, the play of light skimming the surface picks out numerous vertical scratches. The natural first reaction is to look for engravings, abstract examples of prehistoric art. Yet the sheer number of the scratches is something of a surprise, as is their height (some of them reach almost 10 feet). In fact, the marks have been left behind by the claws of the bears who first lived in the cave. During the winter, they took

Opposite:
The Great Ceiling.
A bison's head (Height = 45 cm / 18 in).

shelter deep in the galleries where they hibernated. Doubtless an inbred habit common to a variety of species led the animals to stand up against the cave walls to sharpen their claws.

Because the period of hibernation was fairly long, the place selected for this lengthy state of lethargy had to be laid out as comfortably as possible. Digging into the clay with their powerful paws and turning round and round countless times, the bears made lairs the size of their sleeping bodies and it was in this nest-like dip that the animals huddled throughout the winter. Because the cave is a fossil, the lairs have converged, making the ground resemble a lunar landscape. The trench dug out to provide access to the "Great Ceiling" uncovered the

layer of sediment moved and worked by these animals and led to the discovery of a few bones. After research, the remains showed that the cave had been occupied by three different species.

While on the subject of the bears, it has to be said that they had already abandoned the galleries by the time man arrived to decorate the walls and roof of the cave.

Overleaf:
The Via Sacra. *Three mammoths from the "frieze of five". The young animal on the bottom right is unusual in that prehistoric artists usually depicted adults with enormous secondary attributes (tusks, antlers, horns etc.) (Overall length of engraving incl. all 3 mammoths = 170 cm / 5 1/2 ft).*

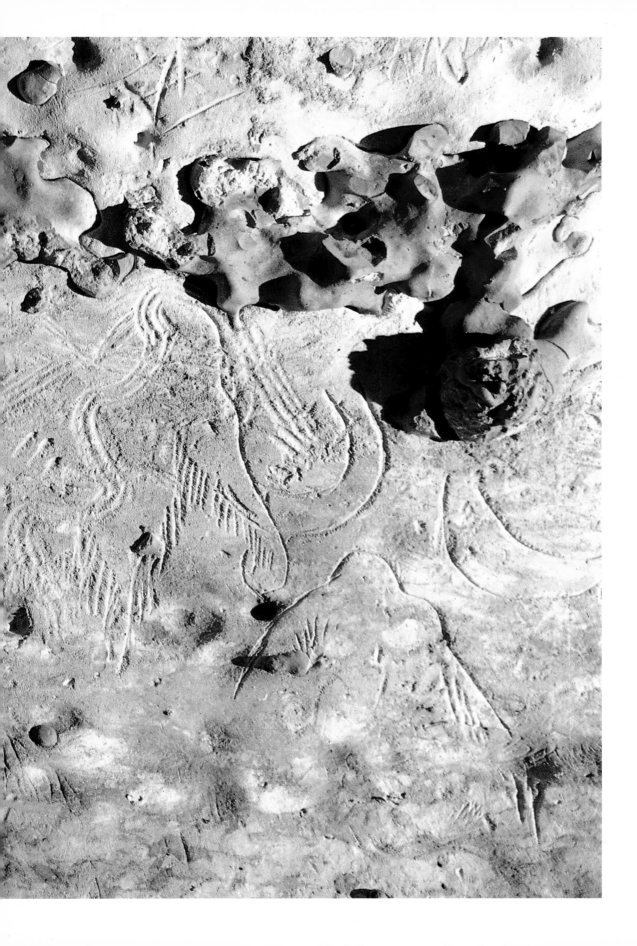

Henri Breuil Gallery. *A rhinoceros in the frieze. This drawing shows quite clearly that the artist was used to seeing such animals. The reverse slope of the upper horn is characteristic of an old animal. (L =110 cm / 3 1/2 ft).*

PREHISTORIC ART

Several thousand years after the disappearance of the bears, man discovered the cave. It was men of the Reindeer Age, Magdalanians, who first dared to advance deep into the maze of passageways. By the flickering light of tallow lamps, they explored the upper gallery from one end to the other. Their perfect knowledge of its layout enabled them to create their art work on the walls and roof of almost two miles of gallery. Yet the decoration is not spread evenly throughout. More than half the paintings and engravings are concentrated within three hundred metres of gallery while the reminaing forty-five per cent are, on the contrary, thinly spread across more than one mile of passages.

MEDIUM AND TECHNIQUES

The surface of the cave walls is of two types. Some of the walls are hard, made up of bare chalk washed by the subterranean river that dug out the gallery; they are full of possibilities. They bear engraved figures and, more particularly, drawings outlined in black. The second type of surface resulted from the chemical alteration of a superficial layer of rock and is soft. Merely pushing the finger into it would still produce a deep inprint, even today. This quality made engraving a necessity, because one can only draw on a base that is harder than the drawing instrument.

The artists, then, had to adapt their technique to the type of surface, although they deliberately restricted themselves to two art forms viz. dra-

wing and engraving. The drawings are all outlined in black and were produced by rubbing a piece of manganese dioxide directly onto the wall or roof. The methods used in engraving are more varied. Depending on the hardness of the base medium, there are lines made with flint chisels or with a bone or wood tool, while in the soft chalk, many of the lines were drawn with the fingers.

Opposite:
Henri Breuil Gallery. *The Head of the Patriarch. The tusks seem to be excessively long but these upper incisors grew throughout the animal's lifetime and could measure more than 3 metres. (Height = 80 cm / 2 1/2 ft).*

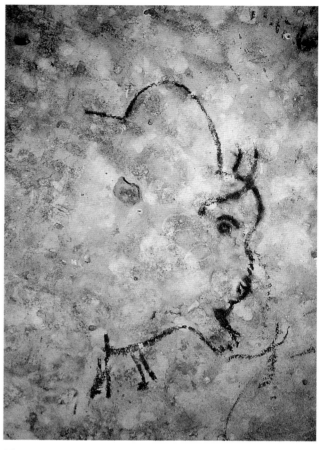

The Great Ceiling. *A large horse's head. Because he could not stand back to look at his work, the artists never had an overall view of what he was doing. This no doubt explains the difference in the techniques used for the body, which is sketched in, and the meticulously-finished head. There are numerous details in the work but its most unusual feature is the attempt to represent a three-quarter profile view (from muzzle to the tip of the ear. Length = 50 cm / 18 in).*

The Great Ceiling. *The front of a bison. Anybody who has ever seen a bison will understand how prehistoric man could be so impressed by the massive size of its forepart. The huge size of the hump compared to the almost insignificant legs is an excellent demonstration of the artist's reaction (Length = 45 cm / 15 in).*

THE FIGURES IN THE GALLERIES OPEN TO THE PUBLIC

Visitors are only shown the area with the largest concentration of figures. In addition to technical problems and the risk of deterioration inherent to a more extended visit, the discovery of all the art in the cave

Opposite:
Henri Breuil Gallery. *An engraving of a horse's head. This subject matter represents only 6% of the total number of animal drawings or engravings, which makes Rouffignac an exception compared to the other caves. (Height = 40 cm / 15 in).*

would take too long (probably ten or more hours).

The three hundred meters of gallery with the greatest profusion of decorative detail are divided into two adjoining passageways. One of them is 195 ft. long and known as the "Henri Breuil Gallery", while the other is a portion of the "Via Sacra".

After moving slowly along 700 metres, the train stops and a dim light plays across the wall of rock to the left. There is apparently nothing to break up the monotony of this smooth, grey surface. Yet after a few seconds, once one's eyes have bvecome accustomed to the light, lines

appear and gradually form the outline of two mammoths. These are the "First Mammoths", the ones which were first seen on 26th June 1956. Deeply engraved in the wall of rock, the two figures are simple but by no means clumsy. In a single, confident sweep, the artist drew a detailed line - the jutting brow, the high-set head separated from the hump on the back by a deep depression, the curve of the rump, all details that define the animal perfectly. The eye of the second mammoth is a natural feature, a flint around which the artist built his work. The subject matter seems to have been obliterated by long, vertical scratches.

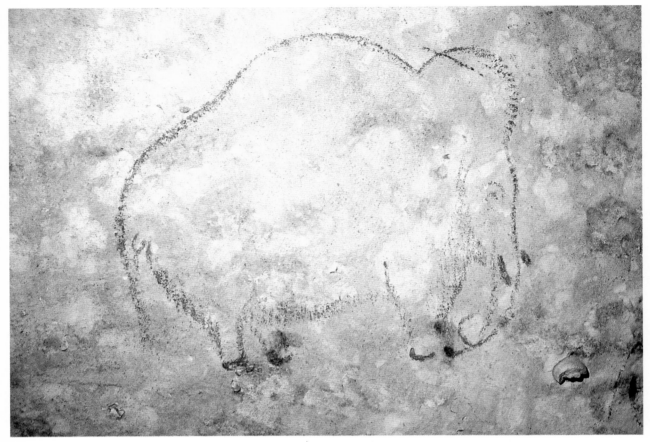

The Great Ceiling. *The « Mammoth with the Anal Operculum ». This piece of work played a vital role in proving the authencity of the cave paintings. Until the results of research into the « deep-frozen » mammoths of Siberia was published, only préhistoric man could have known about this particular anatomical feature (L = 75 cm/2 1/2 ft).*

These are, in fact, marks made with fingers and they preceded the mammoths. There are numerous examples of this art form in Rouffignac, some of them adjacent to animal figures, others set apart, on their own. Their meaning remains an enigma.

On the right-hand walls are another three outlines of engraved mammoths, but they are quickly passed over for three drawings of woolly rhinoceros come into view, again on the wall to the right. These rhinoceros lived in a cold climate and were contemporaries of the mammoths. The drawings form a veritable frieze. Facing towards the right, the three animals follow each other at regular intervals. They have been very carefully drawn, with great attention to detail. The species is perfectly defined and each animal has its own identity e.g. a small broken horn on one, or a horn with an inverted

curve on another. Despite the recent discovery of the cave in Vallon-Pont-d'Arc in Ardèche in which some forty or more drawings of woolly rhinoceros have been identified, they are an unusual subject in Paleolithic art and these three subjects are, therefore, outstanding.

Then we turn again to look at the wall on the left. A third species of animal awaits us - the right profile of a horse. The body is barely distinguishable; only the head has been vigorously engraved. The mane consists of a dozen scratches, while the lower jaw and neck consist of fifteen more. A single long straight line for the nose completes the illustration. The head is set on a slight natural projection on which the ears are engraved. It is surprising for its realism and its aura of a living creature, although one major detail, the eye, is missing.

Immediately before the horse is a roughly-drawn mammoth; opposite it is the "Patriarch". This engraving of the left profile of a mammoth is one of the best designs in the cave. The excessively long tusks suggest that the original animal was very old. Quite apart from the aesthetic quality of the work, it shows the work and skill of the artist. Firstly, he played with the scratches that depict the animal's coat; the variety of form, length and density gives shape and depth to the "face". The artist also made use of the fragile quality of the rock to bring out contrast. A thin, pointed chisel was used for the fur while the enormity of the tusks is suggested by a wide scraping movement effected with a thicker instrument. All the gestures are voluntary and premeditated. Engraving, like a piece of sculpture, is final. The artist cannot erase it or correct it;

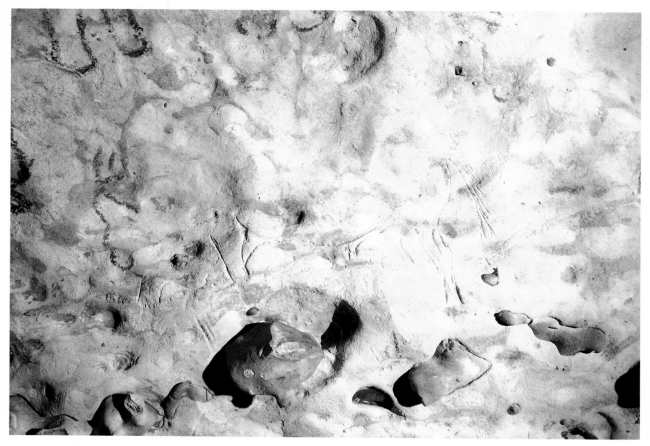

The Great Ceiling. *A bison, half-drawn, half-engraved. This work shows that the technique used did not only depend on the artist's preference but also on the constraints imposed by the condition of the rock below. (Length =70 cm / 2 ft. 2 in).*

he has to achieve the end-result at the first attempt. This means that before starting work, he has to know exactly what he wants to obtain in the way of a result and how he can do it. The premeditated gesture is of vital importance. And it shows the modernity of the skill of these men of the Late Paleolithic Era.

A final step forward and you will see a monumental piece of art work stretching along the right-hand wall - two long herds of mammoths facing each other. There are ten animals in this work, which is over 29 ft. in length. Here, more than anywhere else, the design seems to have been marked by a will to achieve "composition". The wall, which has a band of flint high up and coarse-grained calcite covering the lower section, is unsuitable for painting apart from the central band, hence the decision to paint a frieze.

And although the surface is smooth, it is not flat. It forms two vast concave depressions separated by a mound. The artist studied the characteristics of his background and sought some way of achieving harmony. The two groups of animals face each other on the mound so that each of them is sheltered within a depression. The last animal in each herd is separated from the others. The overall effect is one of total symmetry and there is a perfect balance between composition and the background medium. It is difficult to assess the artistic quality of each of the animals in this painting. The upward spread of calcite has covered more than half the work. In some places, only the outline of the hooves of a few of the animals can still be seen. The presence of these few details suggests that all ten mammoths were originally painted in full. But the

calcite deposit that conceals the base of the frieze also constitutes a proof of authenticity.

It is here, in front of the great "Ten Mammoth Frieze" that the Henri Breuil Gallery ends, near a huge natural funnel. The Gallery was named in honour of the great French scientist who chaired the committee responsible for authenticating the art work in the cave. Visitors then have to retrace their steps to the previous junction before heading off to the left along the "Via Sacra".

Overleaf:
The Great Ceiling. *This is the most complete drawing of a mammoth anywhere in the cave. In the middle of its body, a series of eight "commas" have often been thought to be injuries. Yet there is nothing in the attitude of the animal to support this theory. (Length = 110 cm / 3 ft. 4 in).*

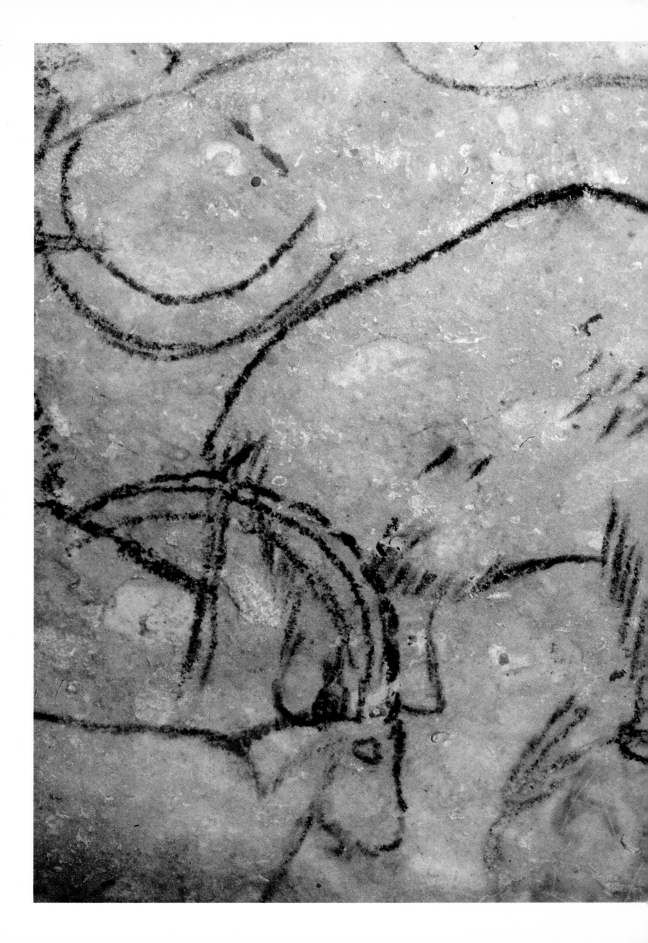

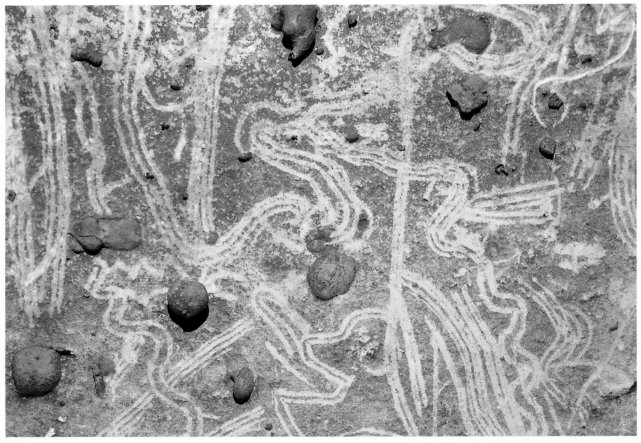

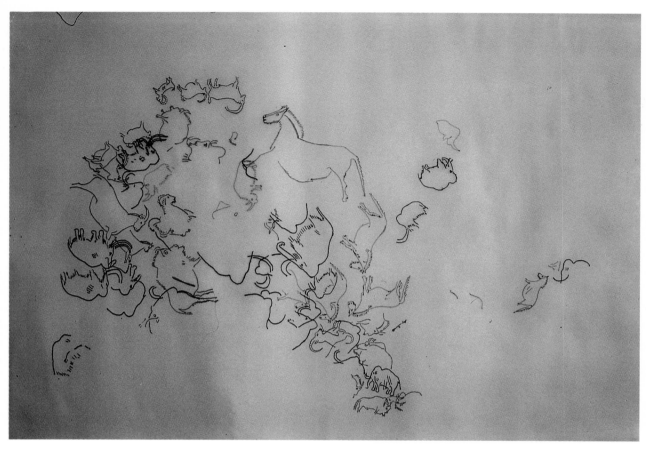

A sketch of The Great Ceiling after the drawing by Claude Barrière (L'Art pariétal de Rouffignac, Picard, 1982).

Opposite, top:
The Via Sacra. *An engraved tectiform symbol. The pad of clay formed on the fingertips has remained in place at the ends of the lines, showing the direction in which the artist "drew". (Length = 40 cm /15 in).*

Opposite, bottom:
Fingermarks forming meanders and snakes. There are numerous caves containing this type of abstract art.

A few yards into this gallery with its bears' dens, there is another frieze, this time of five mammoths, on the right-hand wall. Two groups of two animals are shown facing each other while the fifth mammoth, shown in profile from the right, fills the empty space between the heads of the front two animals. Because of its perfectly central position, this very small animal, probably a young mammoth, increases the effect of symmetrical composition. The surprising feature of this painting is its qualitative imbalan-ce. The two animals shown in profile from the right are very carefully outlined, and the trunk, woolly coat, legs and eyes are shown in detail. The two animals shown in profile from the left, on the other hand, are drawn in a highly simplistic style. Only the vigour of the engraved lines is identical in both cases. One of the mammoths is covered by finger marks. On the cave roof, these numerous, enigmatic marks form an intermingled pattern that does not apparently represent any form or animal. In Rouffignac, there are some five hundred square meters (5,380 sq. ft) of wall and roof covered with such designs. The prehistorians call them interlacing, macaroni, meanders, or snake-like marks.

THE GREAT CEILING

Beyond the Five Mammoth Frieze, the roof becomes increasingly, and regularly, lower so that after a few more yards, the gallery is only 2 ft. 8 ins. high. It was on their hands and knees that the Paleolithic artists continued to advance into the cave, stopping on the edge of a large funnel some 32 ft. deep which led to the galleries down below. This oval-shaped well is more than 30 ft. in diameter at its widest point. It fills one-third of the left-hand side of the gallery shaped like a rolling mill. It was on the remaining two-thirds of the roof, the more accessible area, that the artists painted and engraved, lying on their backs to

An extended view of the Great Ceiling. *Compare this photograph with the sketch of the Great Ceiling and see if you can find the animals featured here.*

do so. The works in the centre of the roof have been badly damaged by the numerous visitors to the cave in centuries past; they, too, crawled into this section. Only the outlines round the edge of the roof are easily visible.

All the herbivorous animals depicted elsewhere in Rouffignac are present here. Mammoths, bison, ibex, horses and rhinoceros seem to be intermingled. Yet the detailed survey carried out by Professor Claude Barrière shows that the apparently disorderly layout is no more than that - a mere semblance of random design. The first outstanding feature is the placing of the horses and ibex. They form two arches round the edge of the chamber. Only the mammoths and bison are to be seen all over the roof, and are usually depicted together. There are several of these mammo-

th/bison groups and they are easy to pick out.

Among the sixty-six animals on the roof, some merit closer attention. On the right-hand edge of the roof is a mammoth above a group of ibex; it has been drawn with an unusual amount of care and attention. The two-lobed trunk, the suggestion of the double upper eyelid and the indication of the diameter of the tusks by means of a double line show that the artist knew the species particulary well. The same goes for the so-called "mammoth with the operculum". Drawn at the entrance to the chamber but at a distance from the concentration of animals in the centre of the ceiling, it has one unusual detail. The artist has drawn in the anal operculum, a horny thickening of the inside of the tail which was brought hard up against the

anus, providing protection against the rigours of the climate.

It is also worth noticing that one of the ibex and one of the horses are represented on scale 1. One occupies the central axis of the ceiling; the other is on the right-hand side, on the edge of the roof. Because there was insufficient space to stand back and look at these drawings, they could never have been seen in their entirety by the artist who drew them. They pose a question as to the purpose of cave art - and go no way towards providing an answer. If the artist himself could not see his work, who could? What was the most important feature of the work - the act of drawing itself or the end-product? The action or the visual attraction?

A bison drawn directly over the top of the well shows the importance that

Beyond the Great Ceiling. *The "Mammoth with the Cheeky Look". A common feature of prehistoric art is the way in which the meticulous attention paid to one particular detail creates the realism of the subject as a whole. Note the difference in the treatment of the eye and the remainder of the animal (Length = 115 cm / 3 ft. 9 ins, including 21 ins. for the tusks alone).*

was attached to the completion of certain drawings. Designed around natural shading that replaces the animal's eye and hump at the back of the neck, only its head is drawn in. The drawing implement slipped along the bison's back, forcing the artist to engrave the remainder. The change of technique seems to suggest a requirement to continue until the drawing was completely finished.

THE DRAWINGS IN THE GALLERIES NOT OPEN TO THE PUBLIC

The vast majority of drawings not shown to the public represent mammoths, and many of them are mere sketches. We shall mention only a few of the more important subjects.

The engraved frieze in the Red Chamber.

The Red Chamber is a short gallery with a very flat roof, covered with natural red clay. Against this exceptional background, an artist has drawn a frieze of seven mammoths. The unusual feature of this piece of work is, firstly, the size of the animals (more than 6 ft. 6 ins) and, more importantly, the process used to engrave it. The lines have been produced by a series of scratches which overlap like roof tiles. By varying their shape, length and density, the artist has suggested the details of the animals.

The "mammoth with the cheeky look".

This mammoth lies beyond the Great Ceiling. As its nickname suggests, it is the the way in which the eye is drawn which attracted the atten-

tion of Father Henri Breuil when it was first discovered. This is the only mammoth in Rouffignac with a circular eye. In order to ensure that the mammoth seemed to be looking in the desired direction, the engraving had to include the tear duct.

Human figures.

It is usual to emphasise the rarity of this subject matter. But it would be more exact to say that it has been treated in a special way. There are fewer engravings of man than of animals, the drawings resemble caricatures, and they are all in one particular spot. All these characteristics are common to the four anthropomorphs in the cave. One is an almost complete figure but is difficult to understand. The other three consist of no more than faces, two of them engraved and the

Beyond the Great Ceiling. *The Pharaoh. The prehistoric artists often played "graphic games" and this bison is a good example. Its horns and hump make it an animal but the vertical forehead, gaze and beard make it half-human (Length = 70 cm / 2 ft. 2 in).*

other drawn. The two engravings, known as Adam and Eve, are opposite each other at the end of a passageway beyond the Henri Breuil Gallery. The drawing is in a narrow passage at the bottom of the well beneath the Great Ceiling. This is the most explicit of the representations and its situation recalls the Well Scene in Lascaux.

Tectiform symbols.

This term is applied to a type of abstract figure that is common in cave art. There are thirteen such symbols in Rouffignac, and they are identical to the ones found in a number of other caves along the Vézère Valley. They are reminiscent of a drawing of rafters seen from side view. Their meaning is totally unknown to us but the fact that they are also to be found in neighbouring sites suggests that they were designed by people who belonged to the same cultural community.

CHRONOLOGICAL TIMESCALE OF THE DECORATION

During the last few centuries, the continuous wearing down of the ground by countless visitors has removed any traces that might have been useful in dating the work precisely. This, though, is by no means unusual and prehistorians are accustomed to taking the comparative approach. By considering the species of animals represented in the cave, the treatment of perspective, and the respect for proportions, the art work in a cave can be placed within its chronological timescale.

In the case of Rouffignac, the animals all lived in our regions during very cold periods. The planes are perfectly staggered and the proportions are exact. Moreover, there is an evident desire to depict details exactly and an attempt at stylisation. These characteristics did not appear until a very late stage in Paleolithic art. Prehistorians are all agreed that the galleries here were decorated between ten and twelve thousand years B.C. The general uniformity of style and technique shows that the decoration was completed within a very short period and that it was the work of a very small number of artists.

WHY WAS THE CAVE DECORATED?

It is easy to describe the art work; it is impossible to understand it. The cave art in Rouffignac, like the decoration in other caves, is now conside-

red as a many-sided phenomenon.

A quick look at the situation of the work within the underground cave and galleries shows that position was not the result of a random choice. In six places, the representations are in the immediate vicinity of natural wells that are linked to lower storeys. Human figures are all in spots that are difficult to reach. Yet this does not mean that the artists always looked for difficulties as regards access and subject matter - indeed, the work in the Henri Breuil Gallery suggests quite the opposite. The layout of the decorated panels indicates that the primitive artists did not work at random or to suit suggestions from their fellows, but that, on the contrary, they knew the topography of the cave like the backs of their hands. Particular spots were selected to comply with what was probably some sort of symbolism in the underground space.

Prehistorians have shown that there is a syntax underlying the apparent disorderly layout of the figures. This is shown by the combinations of species set out on the panels in a given order. The bison/mammoth groups on the Great Ceiling and the peripheral distribution of ibex in the same chamber provide two excellent examples of this. It is as if we were confronted by a veritable coded message.

This art is neither inspired nor descriptive. The artists never depicted their animals or human figures in their natural surroundings. There is no sky, no sun, no moon, no water or vegetation, not even the ground. This could be an expression of some convention, yet it is noticeable that there is not even an implicit reference to such a thing. On the Great Ceiling, the horses' hooves are not in a supportive position and the tips of their tails are lower than their hooves. In other places, the lower part of the mammoths' bodies consists of no more than a suggestion of a long coat hanging down into empty space. Many of the animals are depicted by a mere outline or some prominent feature of their anatomy. Despite the realism of certain anatomical details, everything suggests that the aim was not to depict animals with any sense of realism. In an atmosphere that is steeped in an

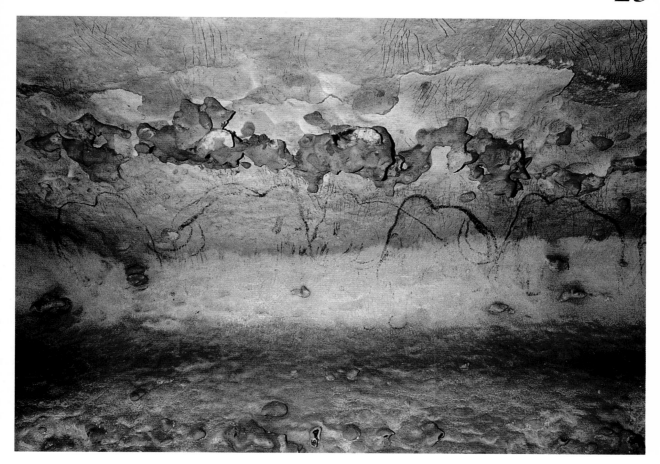

Henri Breuil Gallery. *The centre of the Ten Mammoths Frieze. This is probably the best example of the care paid to composition by Palaeolithic artists. The painting is laid out from the upper seam of flint. The mammoths come together on the natural convexity of the cave walls and the heads of the two "leaders" are set out in a perfectly symmetrical fashion. This shows that the artists were capable of undertaking very real mental projection before beginning their work.*

impression of serentiy, the subject seems to be immaterial. Perhaps the artists were depicting a principle or a concept? Perhaps the animal was nothing but a support for some form of symbolism? Perhaps...?

Similar structures have been found in various decorated caves in Périgord, the Pyrenees and Cantabri and they show the durability of this coded system - it lasted for several thousand years. They also prove that such art work was of great importance to hunting peoples during the Magdalanian Era.

It is then very tempting to ascribe beliefs or rites to these people, basing our hypotheses on what we know of groups living in similar conditions today. And so we arrive at ideas of magic, initiation rites, totemism, shamanism etc. Yet although we are now in a position to identify the existence of certain "spiritual" preoccupations through graphic art and although we have a few notions of the prehistoric economy or some of the technological prowesses of the times, we are totally ignorant of all the rest. What customs did they have? What were their beliefs? What were their legends, and how was their society organised? What occasion led to the drawing of this figures?

All these questions remain unanswered. So we shall retain the suggestions put forward by André Leroi-Gourhan who, after considering nothing but the information that has come down to us and the details of a code that resulted from rigorous study, assimilated the phenomenon with "the expression of a concept over the natural and supernatural organisation of the living worlds.. which could be one and the same thing in the Paleolithic mind".

The Great Ceiling. *A drawing of an ibex. The artist has built up his work to suit the contours of the rock beneath. One protruding section coincides with the thigh; another with the muscle on the neck. This is a veritable piece of prehistoric "paging". (Length = 50 cm / 18 in).*

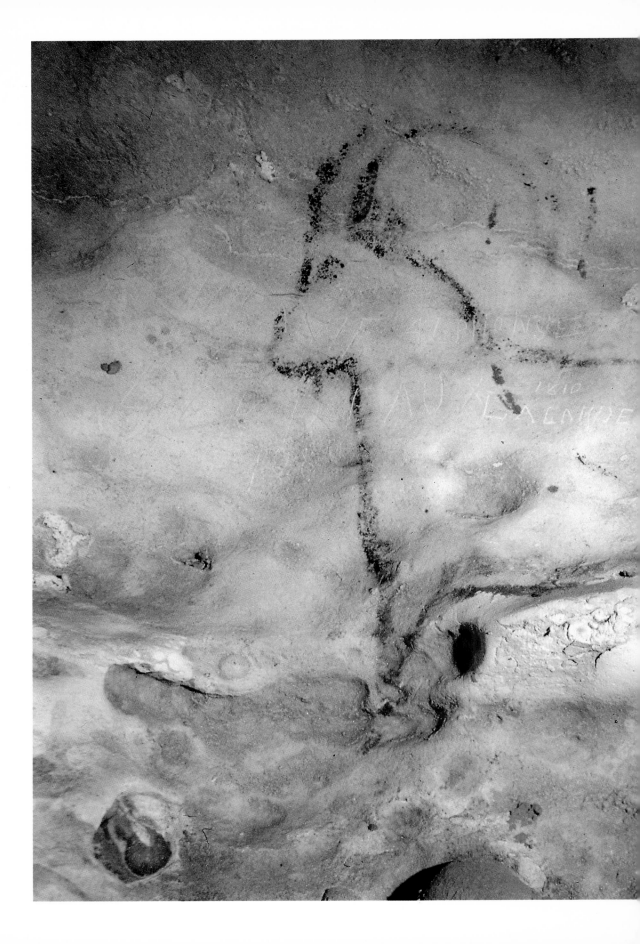

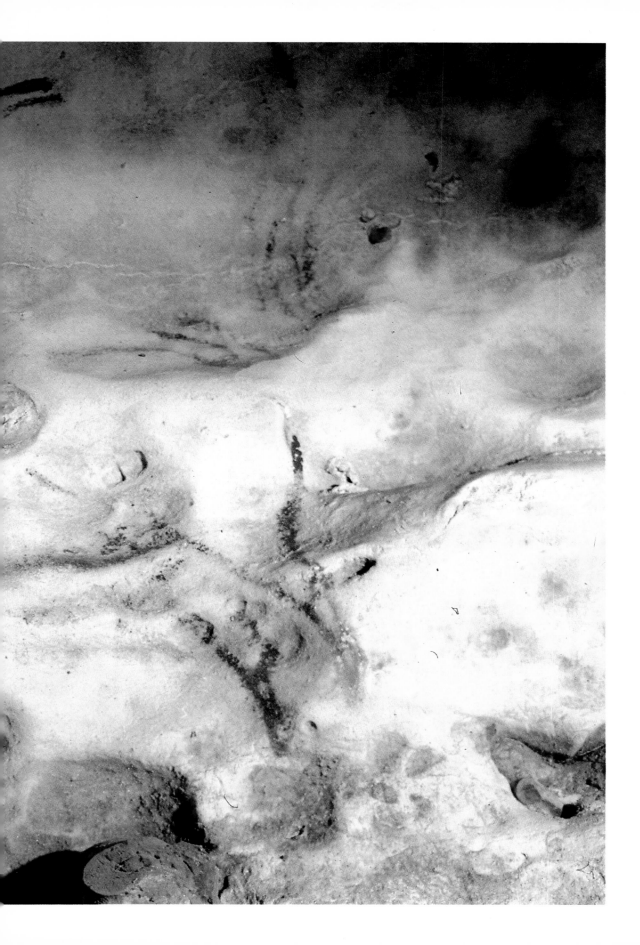

PORTRAIT OF AN ARTIST

Identity form
SURNAME : Homo
FORENAME : Sapiens Sapiens
Height : 6 ft.
EYES : ???
HAIR : ???
ADDRESS : ???
RACE : Cro Magnon
SOCIO-CULTURAL CATEGORY:
Magdalanian
PROFESSION : Artist

The few skeletons or human bones found in various prehistoric sites make it possible to imagine the physical appearance of the men responsible for the works of art in the caves. Everybody has heard of Cro Magnon Man (Homo sapiens sapiens). Generally speaking, the anthropometric observations of Cro Magnon types lead to the opinion that he was a modern man who resembled us.

Early in the century, it was shown that Cro Magnon man had several levels of industry viz. Aurignacian, Solutrean, and Magdalanian. The cave art in Rouffignac is part of the Magdalanian Era which gets its name from the La Madeleine site four miles upstream from Les Eyzies on the right bank of the Vézère.

THE MAGDALANIANS

Living in our regions between 15,000 and 8,000 years B.C., they were first and foremost hunters and harvesters. It is difficult to say precisely which plants, berries or mushrooms were part of their daily diet. On the other hand, the large number of animal bones discovered on sites where they had lived gave precise information about the species they hunted. They were all large herbivorous animals such as horses, bison, mammoths (although there were fewer mammoth bones) and smaller species such as hares and partridge. Yet one animal outstrips all the others - the reindeer. Overall, its bones account for more than 80% of any discoveries. This is why the Magdalanian Era is also known as the Age of the Reindeer. This animal was a major supplier in its own right. In addition to its flesh, it provided clothing and the raw materials for tools and weapons. Fearsome hunters, Magdalanian Man was also an artistic genius, hence the wide variety of tools. The usual range of flint chisels, scrapers, and drills was completed by a whole series of tools made of reindeer bone and antlers e.g. needles, spear tips, and two major inventions - the harpoon and the sling. Most of the bone tools were decorated with animal designs consisting of engraved outlines. Just as numerous are the technico-stylistic references that indicate the art of the Age of the Reindeer and, even better, indicate precisely which level of the Magdalanian it belongs to.

As to their housing, the people lived at the foot of a well-situated overhang of rock, at the mouth of a cave, or more simply in the open air, in huts or tents.

This is all we know about the artists of Rouffignac for the Magdalanians did not live at the mouth of this cave. Did they live nearby? Did they come here for this special purpose or during a period of seasonal migration? Nobody can tell us for the moment. This is yet another reason to remain prudent in our attempts at interpreting what we see.

A LIST OF WORKS

Mammoth,
number 157, percentage 61.8%
Bison,
quantity 28, percentage 11%
Horses,
quantity 17, percentage 6.7%
Ibex,
quantity 12, percentage 4.7%
Rhinoceros,
quantity 10, percentage 3.9%
Bears,
quantity 1, percetage 0.4%
Human figures,
quantity 4, percentage 1.6%
Tectiform symbols,
quantity 13, percentage 5.1%
Snake-like symbols,
quantity 6, percentage 2.4%
Unexplained symbols,
quantity 6, percentage 2.4%
Total
quantity 254, percentage 100%

HOW IMPORTANT IS THE ART WORK IN ROUFFIGNAC?

None of the decorated caves summarises the entire evolution of Paleolithic art. The phenomenon stretched over a period of two hundred centuries and, to us today, the decoration of each cave would be the equivalent of a flash of lightning, for it took only a few years or decades.

Starting from schematic, and often clumsy, sketches, Palaeolithc art tended towards realistic representation of part of the animal kingdom. It is usual to take as examples of the horses in Pech Merle (in the village of Cabreret in the Lot). The backs and bellies of these animals are two enormous curves, their legs are short and slender, and the head is only two inches long for a total length of 5 ft. 4 ins. The horse is a flagrant example but generally speaking the absence of correct proportion and persepctive shows how old these drawings are and how much progress there was still to be made. These figures were drawn 20,000 years ago at a time when people had already been practising graphic art for nearly 10,000 years.

From then on, events gathered momentum. In Lascaux, 3,000 years later, the progress is evident. The essential volumes are indicated and the joints and details of the hooves are also visible. Yet there are still errors as regards proportion and there is a bi-angular view which led to what Father Breuil described as "twisted or semi-twisted perspective" depending on the extent of the deformity. By skilful use of paint, though, the artists began to get closer to an exact representation of their subject.

It was with the art of Font de Gaume (Les Eyzies) 2,000 years later that Prehistoric art entered its Classical period. The harmony in the shapes of the bodies, the exactness of proportions, and the respect for pers-

Opposite :
The Great Ceiling. *The head of an ibex. This is one of the works showing the greatest degree of realism. The artist illustrates the anatomical details while, at the same time, depicting the animal's nature stance (Height = 60 cm/21 in).*

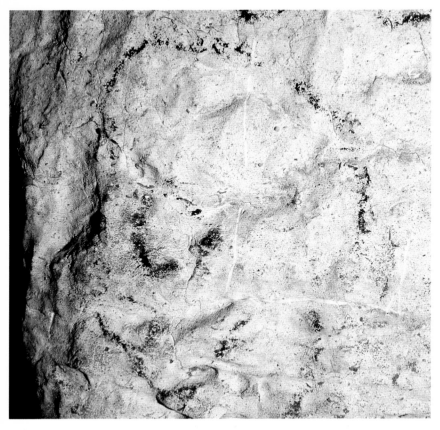

In the well beneath the Great Ceiling. *A representation of a human face framed by two bison. There is an obvious difference between the way in which the human figure and the animals have been treated. (Head, Height = 24 cm / 10 in).*

pective allied to skilful painting techniques gave the animals realism and life. Another leap forward 1,000 years and the Magdalanians discovered Rouffignac.

By then they had acquired such mastery over perspective and they showed such skill in the use of synthesis that it took them only a few lines to sketch in their subject matter. The Patriarch, the Rhinoceros Frieze or the bison and horses on the Great Ceiling all prove their craftsmanship. This is the result of two hundred centuries of technical inventiveness. Details are appositely indicated. The compositions are well-balanced. Everything indicates the know-how of real professionals yet the work is more austere. Efficiency takes pride of place. There is a foretaste of the pure symbolism of later years, with less emphasis on display and a push forward towards abstract art.

CONSERVATION AND TOURISM: THE PROBLEMS AND THE SOLUTIONS

Here we are, faced with documents more than 13,000 years old that have suffered damage on numerous occasions. There is nothing abnormal about that. There was no reason why the prehistoric figures should escape the aging process.

The conservation of this type of art depends mainly on the natural balance within the environment, with the key factors being the climate underground and changes in the condition of the walls of rock. A cave, though, is also subject to the constraints placed upon it by its external environment. Climatic changes, modifications in plant cover, the use of the soil for farming and many other parameters are very influential. They cause variations in temperature, the formation of

draughts (which can sometimes be abrasive), condensation and trickles of water. In many cases, the consequences have been fatal, causing the upper surface of the rock to flake or wash off, the formation of a calcite film or stalagmites, and deposits of natural dust. This means that only a miracle can ensure the conservation of such works of art and that, contrary to widely-held beliefs, they will already have suffered extensive damage even before they are discovered.

A degree of vigilance is therefore vital if we are to protect the caves that we have found and this has led to the implementation of a number of conservation measures which may affect access for visitors or researchers. The number of people allowed into the caves every day, the times of day (or of the year) at which such visits are authorised, and a reduction in the power of the lighting used are the main factors.

The installation of an electric-powered train is part of this movement towards making visits as discreet as possible. This means of transport quickly appeared to be particularly useful for the conservation of the cave and the art works that it contains. Thanks to the train, many of the potentially damaging aspects of visits by large numbers of people can be avoided. The soil is not tamped down by people on foot, visitors are always at an adequate distance from the cave walls, and the quantities of airborne dust, germs or spores are kept to a minimum. Moreover, because the engine runs off a battery, all fixed lighting has been replaced by the mobile light provided by the train's headlights. The duration and power of the lighting has thus been considerably reduced on a day-to-day basis. This being so, the opening of Rouffignac to visitors has not caused the conservation problems usually resulting from such a move.

THE REMOVAL OF GRAFFITI

We have to admit that, although the archaeological interest of the cave is immense, the cave also has its own history which has been revealed to

The Great Ceiling. The great mammoth. If you look at this photograph very carefully, you will be able to see a mammoth which has been completely covered by the soot from candle flames. A large number of the works on the Great Ceiling were in this conditions when they were discovered in 1956. (Length = 1.40 m /4 1/2 ft).

The Great Ceiling. The great mammoth. A comparison between this photograph and the previous one shows the effectiveness of the cleaning operation undertaken on the Great Ceiling. (Length = 1.40 m /4 1/2 ft).

those who have been visiting it for the past four centuries by the abundance of literature on the subject and by the presence of inscriptions marked in candle smoke. There has been some discussion as to whether these graffiti should be removed. In the 1960's, prehistorians proved that the cave could be cleaned but, because they could not take any risks, they had to begin by a meticulous study of all the surfaces likely to be suitable for this type of work. The idea was shelved and it was not until 1989 that the operation was finally undertaken with the assistance of the engineers and technicians from the laboratory run by the Monuments Historiques, by agreement with the body's upper council.

The purpose of the work was twofold. It was designed firstly to rehabilitate the work and, secondly, to preserve the evidence of the cave's sad history. This is why the work was restricted to cleaning off the graffiti that had been added over the top of prehistoric figures. Moreover, since the work could not be carried out along

The electric train. The conservation of this site is being ensured thanks, mainly, to this small train. The cave is not trampled by visitors' feet, the lighting is not continuous and the number of visitors allowed into the cave every day is limited.

outlines, the graffiti had to be cleaned off to each side of the original lines. Only a restoration expert could undertake such work and several periods

were necessary before the Ten Mammoths Frieze and the Great Ceiling were restored. The fragility of the cave walls and roof, and the com-

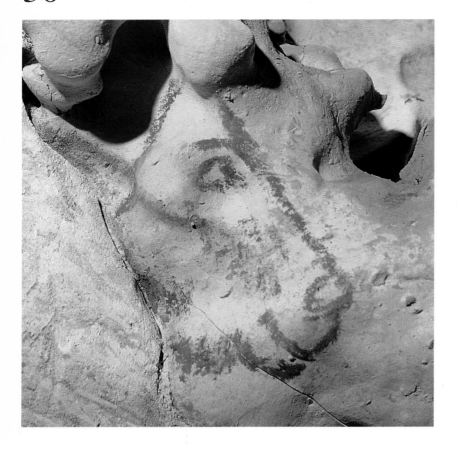

position of the rock, made it impossible to use chemicals. Instead, it took cotton buds, demineralised water compresses, observation on the part of several people and immense patience in order to remove the unwanted additions, slowly but surely.

THE FARMER, THE POTTER AND THE OTHERS

The artists of the Magdalanian Era were only the first people to use the site; they were not the last. More recently, between 7,000 B.C. and the Gallo-Roman period, the cave and its mouth were used on several occasions. The hill to the left of the entrance provides a major indication of the stratigraphic features left by these successive periods of occupation. The hill is of great archaeological interest and parts of it have been subject to digs. It revealed a wide range of implements, scraps from meals, pollen of varying types, and hearths. It is now concealed behind a wall and protected by a slab of concrete. However, an opening has been made in this construction to show the various levels of occupation in the post-glacial period.

The Mesolithic Era was a transitional period between the Palaeolithic and Neolithic; it is represented by Sauveterrean and Tardenoisian cultures. The Iron Age is present in tools from the Hallstatt period. The sequence ends with the Gallo-Romans and mediaeval users.

THE MESOLITHIC ERA

At the end of the Ice Age some 9,000 years ago, the extension of the forest pushed back the great herbivores of the tundra. A new civilisation was born as a result of this environmental change. The new race of

A stratigraphic cross-section. The cave mouth was occupied on several occasions from the Mesolithic Era to the Iron and Bronze Ages. Digs carried out from 1957 to 1962 by Professor C. Barrière revealed the various archaeological levels corresponding to these periods of occupation. The alternating layers of charcoal and virgin sediment are clearly visible here.

humans no longer sought sanctuary in the cave but, instead, lived at the cave mouth. They were still hunters and they cooked stag and wild boar; animal bones can still be found today round the prehistoric hearths. Yet they also entered the cave, seeking flints they used for some of their tools. The scrapers, gravers, punchers and other such implements were still very much in daily use but they also had a new tool - the "sickle-knife". The knife was mounted on a handle and used to harvest grasses. The seeds were ground down into flour which supplemented the daily diet. Times changed; so did habits. This was the start of domestication, and man began to keep dogs. In fact, far from being the simple predator who was totally dependent on his environment, man had begun to control Nature. Crop-farming and stock-breeding were about to come into being. The temperate climate, different technical skills, a new form of economy, and a different social organisation no longer justified the occupation of the cave mouth. People moved away to settle elsewhere.

THE IRON AND BRONZE AGES

Having become farmers, then potters and, 5000 years ago, metal-workers, our ancestors rediscovered the cave mouth and turned it into a "graveyard". Eight skulls (they were almost complete) were uncovered in a space of just five square metres (54 sq. ft.). The skulls, which have a low dome, are an indubitable indication of the development of modern man.

More recently still, at the very beginning of the first millennium B.C, during the so-called Hallstatt period (Early Iron Age), their successors cremated their dead at the mouth of the cave and turned the cave itself into a graveyard.

The ashes of the deceased were scattered over an area stretching from 50 metres (162 ft.) outside the cave to 500 metres (1,620 ft.) inside. These ritual remains were discovered in twenty different spots. They consisted mainly of human ashes accompanied by a few fragments of pottery and ani-

A lance and buttons. Discovered at a distance of 450 m/488 yds, from the cave, these items were part of a burial offering and are thought to date from the Iron Age (Hallstatt period).

mal offerings. Among the burial items were ashes accompanied by a lance and seven bronze buttons.

THE OTHERS

The prehistoric period was finished and the craft of the great huntsmen had died out. The population had become sedentary. They built villages and their economy was based on a system of barter. The cave-sanctuary had fallen into oblivion; the cemetery and graveyard, too, were forgotten. Yet a number of legends of unknown origin maintained a pregnant, one might almost say disturbing, atmosphere in this particular spot. Thereafter, only a few reckless visitors risked a visit to such a sombre place. Some, in order to exorcise the fear gripping the pit of their stomachs, wrote their names on the cave ceiling or walls. Then one day, early in the summer of 1956...

USEFUL BIBLIOGRAPHICAL REFERENCES

Rouffignac
BARRIERE (C.), L'Art pariétal de Rouffignac, Ed. Picard, 1982.
NOUGIER (L.R.) - ROBERT (R.), Rouffignac, Ed Sansoni, 1959.
NOUGIER (L.R.), Rouffignac, la Grotte aux Cent Mammouths. 1978.

Prehistoric art
NOUGIER (L.R.), L'art de la préhistoire, Coll. Encyclopédie d'aujourd"hui. La Pochothèque, Hachette, Paris 1994.
ROUSSOT (Alain), L'art préhistorique. Editions Sud-Ouest, Coll. Sud-Ouest Université, Bordeaux 1994.
LEROI-GOURHAN (A.), L'art pariétal. Langage de la préhistoire, JEd. Jérôme Millon.

Prehistory
WHITE (Randall), Préhistoire. Editions Sud-Ouest, Bordeaux 1993.
SURMELY (F.), Le mammouth. Géant de la préhistoire. Solar

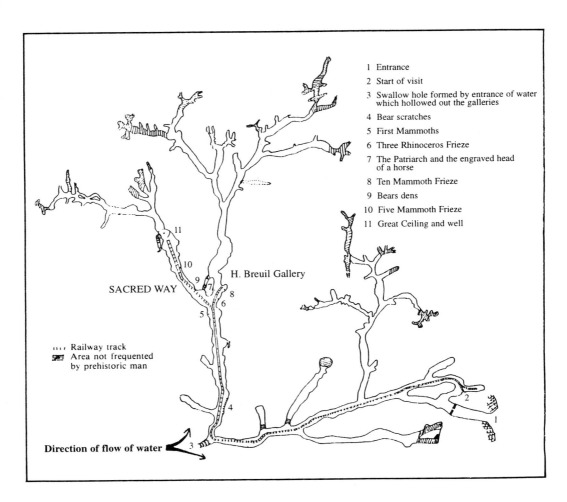

1 Entrance

2 Start of visit

3 Swallow hole formed by entrance of water
   which hollowed out the galleries

4 Bear scratches

5 First Mammoths

6 Three Rhinoceros Frieze

7 The Patriarch and the engraved head
   of a horse

8 Ten Mammoth Frieze

9 Bears dens

10 Five Mammoth Frieze

11 Great Ceiling and well

H. Breuil Gallery

SACRED WAY

···· Railway track
▨▨ Area not frequented
    by prehistoric man

Direction of flow of water ◄

TABLE OF CONTENTS

Front cover:
Two mammoths facing each other. This theme is repeated fifteen times on the cave walls. It is usually described as a confrontation although the attitude of the animals does not suggest any aggressivity. (Length = 50 cm / 18 in).
Back cover:
Scratches made by bears. The mark of the five claws can be seen very clearly; their average width is 25 cm. The highest marks are 3 meters above ground level. Marks like these can be seen from the cave mouth onwards and are repeated in every gallery.

© Copyright 1995 – Editions Sud Ouest. Ce livre a été imprimé par Pollina à Luçon (85) - France. La photocomposition est de Sud Ouest à Bordeaux. La photogravure est de Photogravure d'Aquitaine à Bordeaux. La couverture a été tirée par l'imprimerie Raynard à La Guerche de Bretagne (35), et pelliculée par Pollina.
ISBN : 2.87901.185 X - Editeur : 458.01.04.03.95. - N° d'impression : 67437 - B